I0505374

7 Stock Market Strategies

...that Work!

*Proven Strategies for Making Money
from the Stock Market*

Richard Nicholas

DISCLAIMER

© **Richard Nicholas, all rights reserved.**

No part of this e-book may be reproduced, stored, or transmitted in any form or by any means including mechanical or electronic without prior written permission from the author.

While the author has made every effort to ensure that the ideas, statistics, and information presented in this eBook are accurate to the best of his/her abilities, any implications direct, derived, or perceived, should only be used at the reader's discretion. The author cannot be held responsible for any personal or commercial damage arising from communication, application, or misinterpretation of information presented herein.

Nothing in this book constitutes financial, legal or other advice. It is very important that you do not rely on any of these strategies without investigating them and understanding the risks involved. All investing and trading involves risk and you can lose money even when you're doing everything right.

You can find video training on these strategies at
www.getstartedwithstocks.com

Contents

You can get free downloads (including video summaries of the 7 strategies) at www.getstartedwithstocks.com

INTRODUCTION

If you're reading this book there's a good chance that you're interested in making money from the stock market. You may well be trying to find the right strategy.

You may well find, as I did when I was looking to invest, that there's far too much information on the internet to digest, much of it confusing and some of it actually conflicting.

I wasn't interested in choosing individuals stocks (which felt like hard work). I wanted to know (and do) what had been proven to work in the stock market over time. And I wanted a step by step guide describing what to do.

This book is a result of considerable reading, years of investing and trading in the markets, a lot of experimenting, a lot of money invested in training courses and quite a bit of money lost when things went wrong. Over the course of the last 15 years I've come to realise that there a number of different strategies for making money. Lots of them are good. Some are terrible. The ones in this book are those that I have found to work and which I have found have needed very little active involvement in order to work.

No one wants to be sat in front of a computer screen staring at charts. All seven strategies set out in this book take less than an hour a week. Some take less than an hour a year.

I can't claim credit for "discovering" any of the strategies in this book – they've all been tried and tested by many, many people before me.

When you find the one that works for you, you'll find more information about it in the final chapter of this book, which contains useful resources and further reading.

What is the "right" strategy?

Whilst there's no "right" or "perfect" strategy for investing or trading in the stock market - there are at least some that have at least been tested over time and have been shown to work. That applies to all of the strategies in this book.

The right strategy is likely to be the one that is "right" for you. Some require virtually no effort at all (see strategy 2), others very little effort (strategies one and three), whilst others require you to keep a slightly closer watch on the markets.

All of the strategies have their advantages and their downsides, so it's worth working out what's the right strategy for you. In particular it's worth working out if you want to ignore the markets (and your investments) most or all of the time, or if you want to pay a keener interest in them. Higher returns are on offer if you're prepared to invest the time required to get to know the right skills, but it does take a little bit more effort. You might well consider that extra effort worth it if the result is to allow you to stop working so hard at your full-time job.

How to use this book

Important note: I am not a financial advisor and can't advise you what you should do with your own money. Please don't treat this as financial advice (or any other sort of advice). If you're feeling cynical as you read this book - then that's a good sign - you should probably be suspicious of anyone when it comes to investing and trading and should do your own due diligence on any strategy that you decide upon.

In this book I plan to reveal everything - the strategies, their upsides and their downsides. Crucially I'll also show you where you can find out more information about them for yourself. None of the strategies are "New" or "Unique" - all have been tried and tested before by someone (and all of them have been tried and tested by the author). Your job, as you read through these pages is to work out what's right for you.

For each strategy I have set out:

1. The Steps involved in the strategy

2. How the strategy makes money

3. The advantages and disadvantages of the strategy (compared to the others in this book)

4. How the strategy manages risk; and

5. A summary of how the strategy "works"

The strategies are deliberately set out from the most passive (buy and hold) to more active strategies, so they should suit beginner and more experienced trader alike. They are progressive and can overlap, so that the "trend spotting" technique in strategy 3 for instance, can be used either by itself or in combination with the moving average strategy (strategy 4) and short selling (strategy 5).

In respect of all of the strategies you may also choose to first "Screen" the stocks or funds that you choose, using a Stock Screener, as set out in Chapter 10.

Having been through the strategies set out in this book you may decide that a particular strategy sounds appealing. I would strongly advise carrying out your own research (I have suggested in Chapter 12 where you might do this), and practicing the strategy yourself in a virtual account. Chapter 12 also sets out where you might find further resources including where you might find a virtual account and how to use a journal to keep track of your trades and their result.

Before starting on this journey however you might well ask – why should you even bother with the stock market as a means of making money?

Why the Stock Market?

If you look at different ways to make a regular income there are many routes that you could choose – investing in property, creating an online (or offline) business, writing books, podcasting, becoming a social media "influencer" or even working for a living – why would anyone choose the stock market?

One reason could be the fact that the transfer of money on any given day traded on the stock market is huge – and constant.

Whether you're aware of it or not money is changing hands, deals are being made and there are buyers and sellers trading on the stock market all day every day. Whenever and wherever you choose to "plug in" to it, it will be there, waiting for you.

If you can learn to make money from it then you don't need any particular qualification or licence, don't need to be in a particular country – all you need is an internet connection and the same techniques that traders have been using for years, in order to make money from the markets.

Another reason is that the stock market allows you to be extremely independent. You're not reliant on (as you might be in property deals), a mortgage broker, estate agent or negotiating a deal with a seller. In fact, you're likely not to need to speak to another human at all! Rather, with an online brokerage account you're simply looking at a chart, making a decision and placing a trade entirely online, in your time and following your rules.

It is this freedom, the fact that an internet connection or mobile phone makes trading possible from anywhere that attracted me to stock market trading.

Whilst I might have been thinking of jet set travelling to foreign countries and palm tree lined beaches – in fact it was the more mundane but more useful reality of realising that I could trade from the train, whilst walking to work or whilst taking children to their various after-school activities that allowed me to realise that this was a side-business that even I could run, in my own time and from anywhere.

Investing vs Trading

There is a distinction that you will pick up in this book – between "Investing" in the market and "Trading" the market. The distinction is significant and each requires a different mindset, although – as you'll see - there are ways that you can combine elements of each if you wish to. Let's look at the distinction between an "Investor" and a "Trader":

- An "**Investor**" typically buys stocks with a view to holding them for the long term – perhaps forever, or until he or she needs to sell to fund retirement. Strategies one, two and three are more like "Investor" strategies. The investor is focussed on the long-term gain and stands steadfast, regardless of drops in the market (and his or her investments). This does mean that, in the short term an investor is tossed wherever the market throws them - so they MUST have a way of dealing with risk – either by way of diversification (strategy one), the constant inflow of dividends (strategy two) or the use of a signal to get out of the market altogether at certain times (strategy three).

- By contrast a "**Trader**", whilst they may plan to go on trading for years, looks to take advantage of the current trend in the market. They are interested in what the market is doing and looks to take advantage of it. Rather than relying on diversification alone, a trader will typically use an order known as a "stop loss" to quickly get out of a losing position and will make sure that the possible gains that they can make exceed the losses that they are likely to make on each and every trade.

Strategies 4,5,6 and 7 in this book are strategies more akin to "Trading" than "Investing".

As you read through the strategies you might have a view as to what type of approach would suit you best – but these strategies are far from exclusive. You may well choose to "invest" a chunk of money that you do not wish to monitor, or which is for the very long term (such as a pension), whilst being willing to risk a smaller amount on "trading" the markets.

Personally, I do a mixture of both – invest some, trade a smaller amount – but you must make up your own mind based on your own needs and level of comfort. The seven strategies are set out below.

Note – there are some terms that might sound unfamiliar (e.g., ETFs, Dividends, Funds etc) which are explained in the glossary section at the end of the book, where you'll find more on all of the strategies. Also, since it comes up a fair bit – when referring to "stocks" in this book I am using the American term, but these strategies can all be used in any market, wherever you are and so, for instance UK investors can safely read "shares" wherever I've referred to "stocks" in this book.

STRATEGY ONE – BUY AND HOLD

Of all the strategies you'll read about in this book, this one is perhaps the most maligned.

Ironically it is also the one that most people follow. That doesn't make it a bad strategy - in fact it can be the perfect strategy for you if you don't want to constantly monitor your investments and want to make minimal changes to your portfolio over time.

The key question perhaps is not so much "how" to follow this strategy (the clue is in the name – this involves buying stocks/funds/ETFs and holding on to them long term) but WHAT to buy and hold. That is the question that it is worth truly asking.

The strategy

The strategy involves:

1. Buying stocks, funds, markets or other assets that you believe will go up over the long term. By buying "index funds" or ETFs you avoid the decision making involved in choosing which individual stocks to buy.

2. Make sure that you include some of each of the four main asset classes: (1) stocks, (2) bonds, (3) commodities (for instance gold and silver) and (4) cash savings.

3. Choose how much of each of the main asset classes you wish to hold as a percentage of the whole (a process known as "asset allocation")

4. Hold that mixture of assets forever, or at least until you need to sell them. Use the cash savings to fund emergency expenses if you need to, but plan on keeping the stocks, commodities and bonds for at least five years.

5. If you have allocated a particular percentage per asset class (e.g., 25% stocks, 25% bonds, 25% gold, 25% cash) then each year, where those percentages have changed (because a particular asset has gone up in value, so might now represent 30% of the portfolio – or has gone down in value so might now represent only 20% for instance), you re-adjust the percentage in each by:

   a. Selling some of what has gone up in value; and

   b. Buying some of what has gone down in value

So that each of the different areas is in the same percentage as at the start.

This "rebalancing" keeps the portfolio in the same assets, in the same percentages, throughout the term. Since buying and selling bonds, stocks and commodities will involve a cost you will want to avoid rebalancing too often. Many buy and hold investors choose once a year as a suitable time to check in on, and re-adjust their investments.

Except for "rebalancing" above, only sell when you either "need" to (because you need the money) or because you've reached your target date for selling.

One, time-tested allocation, suggested by Harry Browne (see "Further Reading") is to invest 25% in each of stocks, bonds, gold and cash. You can replicate this with

- an index tracking fund or Exchange Traded Fund (ETF),
- a bond fund or bond ETF,
- a gold Exchange traded Fund and
- an interest paying savings account.

How does the strategy make money?

This strategy generally makes money on the simple basis that three of the four constituents of the portfolio tend to increase in value over the long term. Stocks, Bonds and Commodities (Gold and Silver) tend to rise in value, compared to cash over the long term.

Why four constituents?

All four assets make money at different times and in different economic cycles. Harry Browne, creator of the "Permanent Portfolio", suggests that the two biggest influences in an economy are interest rates and inflation. Both interest rates and inflation change over time and this gives rise to different situations in which different assets thrive:

1. Inflation

Most of us are used to the price of "things" (houses, holidays, food) going up over time, in other words, increasing in value relative to cash. In periods of inflation commodities such as gold and silver increase in price. Stocks also tend to thrive in periods of low to medium inflation (as most companies can pass on price increases to customers) but stocks do less well if inflation increases beyond a certain threshold.

Bonds and cash both lose value in periods of high or rising inflation, because the value of money declines against the "things" that money can buy.

We have a had a significant period of inflation in much of the world (other than Japan) and certainly in the since the 1930s.

2. Deflation

There are however periods (such as in the USA from 1930-33 and in Japan from 1990-2001) were the price of "things" (property/food/services) have gone down in value.

In these, relatively rare, periods of deflation cash and bonds both do well. That is because, whilst the value of goods and services are all going down, the value of cash is increasing. Similarly bonds, which pay an amount out in cash are more valuable since the amount they pay out is fixed.

Commodities typically fall in price in times of deflation. Some companies thrive in periods of deflation, others fall in value. Periods of deflation are often associated with crashes in the stock market, meaning that stocks typically lose value when there are long periods of deflation.

3. High or rising interest rates

Central Banks use high interest rates to curb inflation. Alternatively, countries may be forced into accepting higher interest rates where a country is perceived to be unable to pay its debts. In periods of high interest rates cash savings receive a boost.

Stocks and bonds all tend to fall as the cost of borrowing money increases costs for many companies and, since the amount that bonds pay out is fixed, bonds are considered less valuable and tend to drop in value. Commodities also tend to fall as a result of high interest rates – albeit they may have risen if the cause of the high interest rates was inflation.

The period from 1970 to 1990 in the UK saw interest rates spike up to 17% from a previous high of around 8%.

4. Low interest rates

Low, or falling interest rates are typically a period when stocks do well. This is because companies find it easier to borrow and invest. Falling interest rates can be good for bonds and for commodities.

By contrast low interest rates mean that anyone with savings will see the rate of return on savings fall.

At the time of writing interest rates in the UK and USA are at the lowest they have been in the last 200 years.

Holding a mixture of these four assets means that, at any one time at least one of them is increasing in value, even if one or more of the others is suffering a decline.

Won't that mean that I am always losing, as well as making, money?

You might think that having one asset increase in value whilst other decreases would mean that they offset one another, leaving you no better off.

In fact however, extensive back testing by Meb Faber in his book "Global Asset Allocation" (see Chapter 12) has shown that having an equal mix of the four assets and re-balancing that mix over time has led to more consistent results throughout different in than most other passive "buy and hold" strategies. Other strategies have beaten it at different times, and some others have matched it, but this mix has held its own in different economic environments. (On this see Harry Browne's book "the Permanent Portfolio" and Meb Faber's excellent "Global Asset allocation" – details of which are in the "Further Reading" chapter),

During the period 1973 – 2013 for example (the dates used to compare strategies in Meb Faber's book) the "Permanent Portfolio" made a nominal (pre-inflation) return of 8.53% a year (or around 4-5% per annum when adjusted for inflation).

Whilst you could have made a higher return over that period by changing the asset allocation (for instance investing more into stocks), returns become less consistent each year, meaning that you are likely to see your portfolio both rise and fall in value much more than with an equal split.

The magic of re-balancing

The annual "re-balancing" of the portfolio (step 5 above) means that automatically you are "selling high" (i.e. selling assets that have gone up in value and are therefore worth more than their initial percentage allocation) and "buying low" – (i.e. buying assets that have gone down in value and are therefore worth less than their original asset allocation). This has the advantage of making the strategy less volatile and leads to better returns with less risk.

Advantages

This is (nearly) the ultimate "set and forget" portfolio. Set it up and (nearly) forget it – just check on it each year to see what's changed and to put it back on course.

If you want to take no further active involvement in your investments then a "buy and hold" strategy might be for you.

Downsides

A "buy and hold" is invested for the long term. Whilst a diversified spread of assets might be expected to increase in value over the long term, there may be periods when one or more assets in the mix falls sharply and could take a long time to return to their former highs.

A typical investor in this strategy, since they are in it for the long term will not use a "Stop Loss" order to get themselves out of the market in the event of a downturn but rather will trust that the historical behaviour of the different assets will mean that losses in one asset will be compensated by gains in another. For that reason, any buy and hold investor MUST seek to reduce risk by way of diversification (holding in a portfolio asset that behave in different ways at different times).

How does this strategy manage risk?

We've looked at how "rebalancing" the portfolio helps to reduce volatility in a portfolio – but the key thing is the initial asset allocation. "Asset Allocation" means deciding, upfront, the amount of money to put into different assets within a portfolio.

Typically, we know that when stocks fall in value, bonds often go upwards. Having some cash in a portfolio means that we can quickly buy stocks if they fall in value offering us a bargain. In the event of rapid inflation on the other hand, bonds and cash are likely to be quickly devalued meaning that we have to rely on a "real" asset, something that is tangible and whose price moves up as inflation increases – something like property or gold.

There are very many different authorities on what a "perfect portfolio" should contain and financial advisors often base the mix on the unique characteristics of an individual, their appetite for risk and their age.

Some time ago Harry Browne came up with what he called the "Permanent Portfolio" that contained an equal mix of stocks, gold, bonds and cash. You can find both the reasoning behind the portfolio (and how it is designed so that at least one constituent should prosper whenever there's high interest rates, low interest rates, inflation or deflation) in Harry

Browne's book "Fail Safe Investing" (in the "Further Reading" section).

More recently Joe Dallio created a similar "All seasons" portfolio that had a similar promise – to work in all seasons, but based on the relative risk of each of the assets in the portfolio. Dallio's asset allocation, which is explained in Tony Robbins' book "Master the Game" and contains more bonds and less cash than Harry Browne.

Whilst you could compare the two portfolios and various others besides (there are many others who have looked at the question of how best to allocate assets for the long term), the most comprehensive book I have read on the subject is also the one with the most boring title. The inauspiciously named "Global Asset Allocation" by Meb Faber compared each of the different portfolios over a period of thirty years.

The Conclusion?

Of all of the different portfolios, tested over a period of 30 years, Harry Browne's and Joe Dallio's "all weather" or "permanent" portfolios gave the most consistent return in different scenarios compared to the (relatively low) risk.

The results of the testing was that the two portfolios acted very similarly. In fact, the differences between those two portfolios were too close to be significant. Both performed better than the other portfolios.

More significant than the difference between those two portfolios and the rest however was the difference between all of the portfolios containing purely "passive" investments (such as ETF's) and those where a fund manager was actively managing the portfolio.

In order to benefit from the strategy therefore you will need to ensure that you are invested in low cost index tracking funds or ETFs.

Regardless of the mix of assets every single portfolio that was passive did better than an actively managed portfolio. The reason being the additional cost of the fund manager meant that even the right mix of assets could not make up for the costs involved.

<u>The message seems to be therefore:</u>

1. If you're going to buy and hold then you need to diversify between assets

2. You'll also need to re-balance each year

3. In terms of the right mix- Harry Browne or Joe Dallio's portfolios look a good starting point and have been well and truly tested.

4. For each of the four assets you can purchase an appropriate passive fund or ETF in each of stocks, gold, high quality bonds and cash (a money market fund, or simply a high yielding savings account)

5. It's not worth paying a fund manager to actively manage funds for you (in fact it would be worth avoiding "active" funds entirely).

Summary of this Strategy:

By Investing in, and holding the right mix of assets you are best placed to ride the storms in any market.

STRATEGY TWO – DIVIDEND INVESTING

In strategy one, the aim of the investor strategy was for the stocks (and other assets) to go up in value. The investor is focussed on capital gains over the long term. That works well if you're saving for the future (e.g. in a pension) but what if you need to make an income from your investments – for instance if you've already retired, or you are looking to your use your investments to help fund your lifestyle? The aim of the dividend investor is purely to make an income.

The dividends may be used and spent (if needed) or re-invested into the same strategy.

Like the buy and hold investor the intention behind this strategy is simply to buy and to hold the stocks.

If you are using strategy one but quite like the idea of making an income then of course you could use this strategy for the "stocks" part of the mix – so as to make an income from that part of your investment.

Even if you are not intending to use the dividends (i.e. you plan to re-invest them) there is a good deal of evidence (see Chapter 12 and "How does this Strategy Manage Risk?" below) that an income-focussed style of investing, where dividends are re-invested, leads to good capital growth at a lower risk than relying on capital growth alone.

The Strategy

This strategy involves:

1. Buying stocks in large businesses that pay higher than average dividends. You can find these using the resources in Chapter 12. Annual dividends, when divided by the stock price are described as the "yield" of a stock. You are looking for the "highest yielding" stocks in your chosen market (which might be the FTSE 100, the S&P 500 or some other index).

2. If you are relying on the dividend to pay the bills then you are likely to want to use your "home" index – i.e. UK investors might use the FTSE 100 as dividends are paid in £ pounds sterling, whereas US based investors might instead prefer the S & P 500 on the basis that dividends are paid in $US Dollars. (If you're planning to reinvest the dividends then you are of course free to choose whichever index you prefer)

3. In order to manage risk, you will need to spread your investment over 10- 15 stocks should be obtained, all in different sectors of the market. This does mean that the stocks chosen might not be the 15 highest yielding in the relevant index (for instance several of the very highest yielding may well be in same sector) – however it is more important that the stocks are spread across different sectors of the market (e.g., retail, finance, commodities, food etc). This is because different sectors are likely to be going up or down at different times

4. All of the stocks should be big businesses (i.e., from the FTSE 100 or S&P 500). You want to know that the

businesses are big enough in size that they are likely to continue to pay a dividend for years to come. Of course, there are no guarantees, but the risk of a smaller company being unable to pay a dividend is significantly higher.

5. Re-invest the dividends until you need them. When you need them take them, but until you do, re-invest for compounded growth.

6. [Optional] As with Strategy one – you might choose to "rebalance" between your 10-15 sectors from time to time to make sure that you do not become too focussed on one sector. (This could happen for instance when a particular sector surges ahead, meaning that the stock price increases much higher than the other stocks that you hold). Stephen Bland in his excellent writing on the Motley Fool about the "High Yield Portfolio" suggested that this might not be worth it – as the costs of buying and selling stocks every year could outweigh the potential benefit.

7. [Optional] Again – not recommended by Stephen Bland in his original writing, but something that you might consider (and which I have used) is having a "Stop Loss" in place in respect of each of your stocks. This is an order to sell the stock, which gets triggered if the stock drops in value by a certain percentage. By setting and leaving a stop loss order in respect of each stock you hold you give yourself some protection against an individual company doing something so outrageous that their stock price drops heavily (e.g. accounting fraud, and environmental disaster, some sort of scandal).

Since you are investing in individual companies, rather than funds or ETFs (as in strategy one), personally I prefer to have a stop loss in place. This means that, if it is triggered, I have not lost too much money and can always reinvest the funds in another company in the same sector.

How does the strategy make money?

Simply by producing a consistent, regular income over time this strategy can be a very effective way of building up wealth. Many studies have shown that a very significant proportion of the income produced from stocks is down to the re-investment of dividends. Compounded over time dividends can be extremely valuable.

Because dividends are taxed as "income" (in the UK at least) you may want to follow this strategy in either an ISA or pension (i.e., a tax-free wrapper).

One of the advantages of investing in income producing stocks is that they tend to be cushioned from steep declines. The reason being that, at times of crisis investors move out of "riskier" assets to assets that are seen as "safer" because they produce a regular income.

Advantages

This strategy offers a regular, fairly reliable income (typically around 4-5% per year, excluding capital growth) – which is particularly useful if you're intending to use it as an income, if you've retired or would like to retire. Quarterly or monthly dividends can give you an independence that the "Buy and Hold" strategy might not give.

This is the ultimate "set and forget" portfolio, even more so than "buy and hold". Set it up and...well – do nothing, ever again except decide whether to accept the income or to keep re-investing it.

You could of course set "Stop losses" so as to prevent stocks falling too far but this is purely optional and some of those who use this strategy (e.g., Stephen Bland of the Motley Fool) suggest instead using no trading at all – no stop losses and no interference EVEN when a stock looks as if it could become insolvent. This is on the basis that, in the long term, meddling only incurs cost and might not improve the situation.

Downsides

As with strategy one, the dividend investor in in the market for the long haul so needs to be able to stay invested and not need to access their capital quickly. The key thing for the dividend investor is that, so long as they are being paid a regular income, they may well not care whether the capital value goes up or down (which it will do as the overall market moves up or down).

How does this strategy manage risk?

Large companies are less likely to become insolvent. Companies in different sectors should act independently of each other (unless the sectors are linked), meaning that it would be unusual for every sector to be equally affected by the same news.

Your initial risk is also reduced with every dividend payment that you receive.

For instance if your portfolio is paying a yield of 5% per year, then the effect of a 5% drop in the stock price is that, at the end of the year you haven't "lost" money (since the drop in the stock price is compensated by the dividend that you have received). After 20 years of receiving a 5% return you have covered the risk of your portfolio entirely, meaning that (ignoring inflation and the other things that you could have done with that money) your "risk" in the original investment has been entirely compensated by the dividends that you have received.

Summary of the strategy:

By seeking dividends from relatively safe, stable investments (rather than seeking capital gain) you reduce your risk over time, and put yourself in a good position to replace your monthly income. By re-investing dividends, you can also use this strategy to produce good capital gains.

STRATEGY THREE – TREND SPOTTING TO MINIMISE RISK

So, we've looked at two very low maintenance strategies. This third one involves only a very small amount of extra work and falls somewhere between being an investor and a trader.

The Strategy

For this third strategy, which is endorsed by a number of different writers, the aim is to take the advantage of being in the market most of the time, but seeking to avoid the big losses associated with a fall in the markets.

This is achieved by setting an indicator to come out of the market when the market is, or appears to be about to fall. To amount to a strategy there needs to be a corresponding trigger to get back in to the market when it is rising or appears about to rise.

You could use different methods to do this, such as, once you have bought your investment, immediately placing a "stop loss" order that sells in the event that your investment falls by 10%. You can usually set this order to rise with the price of the investment so that, as your investment rises the trigger also rises, meaning that you protect your gains as the stock rises.

As soon as the trigger is hit and your investment is sold and returned to cash you would want an alternative trigger – for instance a "stop buy" order that buys back your investment when it goes up by 10% and appears to be, once again going in the right direction.

Using stop losses and stop buy orders in this way starts to put you into the world of trading – but is there any indicator from the market itself that could help know when to buy and when to sell?

This is where you start to look for a trend.

How does the Strategy make money?

This strategy makes money by always being invested in stocks that are "going" up and out of the market when it is "going" down. By applying this strategy to an Exchange Traded Fund that tracks the market you can be in the market as it rises and out of the market when it starts to fall.

One of the ways to make more money in the market is simply to avoid loses. This strategy helps you to do this. How does it work? You could follow these steps

Look at the chart for the overall index (the S & P 500 or the FTSE 100 or another large index)

On the chart, change the settings to "daily" or "weekly" so that you are looking at a long period of time.

Look for the points where the stock price seems to bounce up from the bottom of the chart, like a ball bouncing off the floor. These are where the investment is making "lows"

Look also for the points where the stock price seems to bounce down from the top of the chart like it is bouncing off the ceiling. That is where the investment is making "highs".

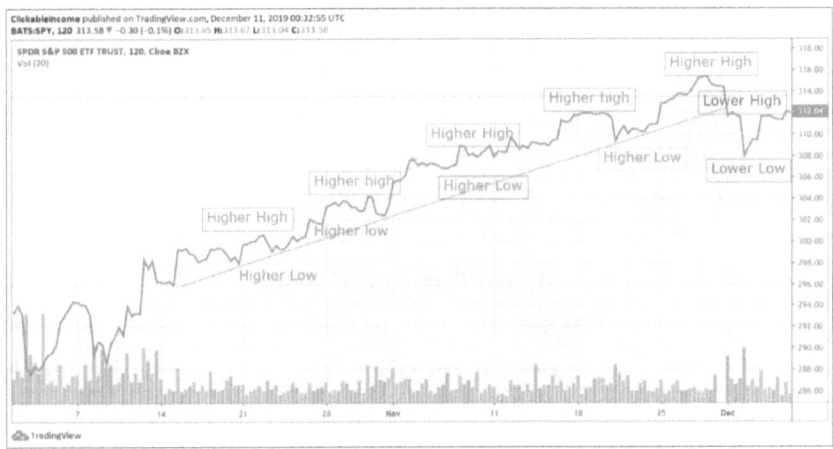

1. What you are looking for is an investment where the "highs" are progressively higher. Effectively you are looking for mountain peaks where each high is higher than the last. You want about three successive highs to each be higher than the last one.

2. You also want the lows to be successively higher – so that each valley is shallower than the previous one – i.e. each "low" is also higher than the previous low.

3. When you have both higher "highs" and higher "lows" (see above) you have an upwards trend. You can buy in to "follow the trend"

4. If you don't have BOTH higher highs AND higher lows you don't have a trend – don't invest.

5. As soon as you get a break in the trend – i.e., the next "high" is lower than the last, or the next "low" is lower than the last – that's a "warning" that the trend may be at an end - consider selling at this point.

6. If the warning above is then confirmed by a lower low or lower high – that is confirmation that the trend is at an end. Sell immediately and wait (holding on to cash) for the next upwards trend.

Advantages

An advantage of this method is that it avoids some of the very big losses in the market. By only being invested in stocks that are going up – you obtain most of the gains from the stock market and avoid the losses that might otherwise wipe out those gains.

If you take a look back at the long term charts and in particular at the large falls in the market (e.g. for the UK and US markets in 2000 or 2007 for instance) you'll likely see that, had you followed this method you would have been out of the market before the big falls, which is a useful benefit to have.

The Downside

The downside is that it does require you to watch a chart of the market that you are invested in. This is a discipline that takes little time and could be once a week or even once a month, but does require some investment of time.

Because you are selling and buying more often than the "buy and hold" investor you are paying fees each time you buy and sell. For this reason, you might not want to have lots of different investments (since you would be paying fees on each one) but rather focus on a particular market, such as the S & P 500 or FTSE 100.

Unlike the trading strategies set out below this is only "one way" so you are either invested when the market goes up, or not invested. You are not making money when the market goes down (but you are not losing money either). With a little more focus and a little more time you could be making a return as the markets fall as well – but at that point you're acting more like a trader!

How does this strategy manage risk?

The strategy manages risk by being out of the market when the market stops rising. Rather than relying on diversification it relies on trend following and being out of the market when the trend changes. You can combine this with "stop loss" and "stop buy" orders to help automate the process.

Summary

By following the overall trend in the market, you can work out when to be invested and when to avoid being invested (and only be invested when the stock market is rising).

STRATEGY FOUR – USING MOVING AVERAGES TO MINIMISE RISK

The Strategy

Very similar to the previous strategy, this strategy looks at the trend of the stock market and keeps you invested in the stock market only when the stock market is going up.

Unlike the previous strategy however, this uses a different tool to looking for "higher highs" and "lower highs" as set out in strategy three. This instead uses a tool that measures how quickly prices are going up or going down. Welcome to the "Moving Average".

Moving Averages Explained

Imagine your child brought results home from school at the end of a school year and when you look at their report you see that they have a "C" average for the year.

That gives you a bit of information about how well he/she is doing, particularly when compared to the previous year. You'd know in broad terms if their work was improving or getting worse, but only when measured over a whole year.

However, imagine if you'd had the benefit of seeing results every month – with the yearly grade being updated every time they did a new test. You'd then have an "average" that moved over time. Knowing that your child received an A in January, February, March and April and then got a "B" in May and then a "C" in June then a "D" in July suggests that something started to happen in May to distract them.

Knowing about a fall in grades shortly after it happens means that you can find out and deal with it earlier. The "average" grade measured over the course of a year would still be a "C" but the average measured monthly would have started to fall – and by July would have fallen below the yearly average.

All that a moving average is then is an average over a certain period in the past – it could be the past 5 days or 5 weeks or even the past year. The longer the period used to measure the average, the slower the average will change.

Typically, a long moving average (e.g., 50 days) depicts a slow-moving line that follows where the price has been, averaged out over a long period.

A shorter (e.g. 20 day) moving average by contrast is much quicker to follow the price and will shoot upwards and downwards as the stock price moves up and down. It will frequently dart above the 50-day moving average as the stock climbs, and dart below it as the stock falls. We can use these crosses to see how quickly the market is moving upwards or downwards.

Rather than just watch the direction, what the indicators are telling us is the speed of change and how quickly the stock price has started to rise or fall.

In particular when both moving averages are sloping upwards and the faster moving average rises above the slower moving average, we know that the stock is rising with gathering momentum. When both are falling and the faster moving average falls below the slower moving average that is a sign that the stock is falling.

In each case this move is often treated as significant as it signifies a shift in the stock's overall direction.

The strategy is then:

1. Buy the market when the 20-day moving average rises above the 50-day moving average.

2. Hold on to the stock for so long as the 20-day moving average stays above the 50-day moving average.

3. Sell the stock when the 20-day moving average falls below the 50-day moving average

4. Stay "out" of the stock (and in cash) until the 20-day moving average again rises above the 50-day moving average (which signals that the stock is gathering pace upwards again, and you can again buy the stock – as per step 1).

How does the Strategy make money?

As with Strategy three, this strategy allows you to avoid the big losses where markets fall. An advantage over Strategy three is that the trigger is more certain – is the 20 days above the 50-day moving average or not? If not – sell.

Advantages

As with strategy three, this has the advantage of being very low maintenance.

It requires very little more work than strategy three, albeit looking on a chart for the moving averages will usually involve a little more patience – a few more clicks in order to get the indicators showing. You can do this on free software such as Tradingview.com or stockcharts.com, on any device, from anywhere – but it does take a couple of minutes longer than simply looking at the chart.

To profit from the strategy you do need to do this consistently (this could be daily, weekly or even monthly, but does need to be done regularly)

This extra work might seem trivial (and it is) but the only strategy that will be successful for you is the one that you are prepared to follow. If the extra couple of minutes means that this is not something that you will do, then don't do it – use one of the previous strategies instead.

Downsides

This strategy does require a more active interest in the market than the first two strategies. Because you are buying and selling more often than in strategies one and two it would make sense not to have a large number of investments but rather focus on one or two funds that track a large market (such as the S&P 500 or the FTSE 100).

As with strategy three – with this strategy you're only making money when markets go up (but on the other hand you're staying out of the market when markets fall).

How does this strategy manage risk?

The moving averages are indicators that show how quickly the market is moving in your favour. By selling when the trend starts to reverse this strategy allows you to avoid large falls.

Since the indicators always follow the price however – they cannot predict or avoid very sudden falls in the market, so if you do use this strategy it is still worth having a stop loss.

<u>Summary</u>

Like Strategy three – by working out which way the stock market is "going" you can place yourself in front of rises and set trades to trigger if your prediction is correct. By watching when moving averages cross (upwards or downwards) you can make sure you are only in the market as it rises.

STRATEGY FIVE – ADDING SHORT SELLING TO FOLLOW THE TREND IN EACH DIRECTION

Strategies 1-4 have been focussed on holding on to and making money as stocks or markets go up in value. Strategies 3 and 4 have also brought in the concept of being out of the market when the market falls.

Strategies 5, 6 and 7 include an additional element – making money when stock markets fall – "shorting" the market. With this strategy you've well and truly crossed over to the world of trading (welcome!)

The Strategy

By combining strategies three and four we can:

1. Look for markets or sectors that are making higher highs and higher lows (trending upwards as per strategy three). Note – in order to do this, you're going to want to have a list of stocks or funds that you can explore. (See Chapter 8 on "Screening for stocks")

2. Where you find them (and you'll likely find lots of them), look for those where they have formed a peak (a higher high) and have retreated from that peak. For those

where that is the case – look at the Moving Averages (as per strategy four) to see if the 50-day MA has crossed **above** the 200-day MA.

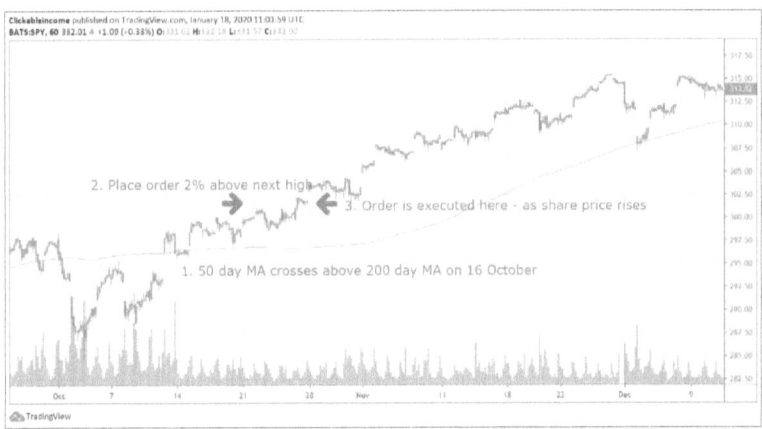

3. Where both those signals are present (see step one in the above diagram), place an order to purchase the relevant fund or stock IF the fund or stock hits a price slightly above (e.g., 2% above) the previous high (step two in the above picture). This order is known as a "stop" order. Depending on your broker it might be described as a "Buy to Open" order (since you are buying to open the trade). The reason for this extra 2% is purely to ensure that the trend is real and likely to continue in the same direction.

4. Once you have placed your order (to enter the trade) it may not be executed straight away or at all. If it is not executed within a month then cancel the order and look for another stock.

5. If the order is executed (step 3), immediately place a stop loss under the purchase price of the stock (e.g. 5%

below) and raise that stop loss as the stock or fund moves higher. There is no need to sell the fund or stock at this point, but rather keep moving the stop loss up as the stock or fund goes up in value. You are making money by following the upwards trend and moving your stop loss order up. You want to stay invested for as long as the trend continues.

6. At some point either your stop loss is likely to be triggered (in which case you will automatically exit the trade), or the trend will come to an end, making a lower high or lower low. At this point sell the stock by placing a "sell to close" order at the market price.

Shorting stocks

All of the above steps also apply to looking for stocks or funds that are falling in value too, so the steps for these are:

1. Look for markets or sectors that are making lower highs and lower lows (trending downwards as per strategy three). Note – in order to do this you're going to want to have a list of stocks or funds that you can explore. (Again, see Chapter 9 on "screening for stocks")

2. Where you find them, look for those where they have formed a valley (a lower low) and have started to bounce up again. For those where that is the case – look at the Moving Averages (as per strategy four) to see if the 50-day MA has crossed **below** the 200-day MA.

3. Where both those signals are present, place an order to sell the relevant fund or stock IF the fund or stock hits a price slightly below (e.g., 2% below) the previous low.

Again, this is known as a "Stop" order. It might also be referred to as a "Sell to Open" order, since you are "selling" the stock or fund in order to "open" the trade.

4. If the order is not executed within a month remove the order.

5. If the order is executed, immediately place a stop loss (which might be referred to as a "Buy to Close" order) above the price at which the order was executed (e.g. 5% above the "sell to open" price) and lower that stop loss as the stock or fund moves lower. There is no need to buy the fund or stock, but rather keep moving the stop loss down as the stock or fund goes down in value. Again – you want to follow the trend downwards as far as possible before you are forced to exit the trade.

6. At some point either your stop loss will be triggered (in which case you will automatically exit the trade) or the trend will be broken because the stock or fund makes a higher low or higher high. Once the trend has been broken exit the trade by "buying to close" the stock or fund at the market price.

I appreciate that following a trading strategy from a book (particularly in relation to "shorting" stocks) can seem strange as it's not something that most people are familiar with. Before diving into this strategy with real money it is therefore well worth getting to know and understand how your broker works. When I teach this strategy, I ensure that anyone I teach this to first uses a "virtual" trading account so that they can get comfortable doing this with virtual funds and are not in danger of losing real money simply as a result of not understanding the right buttons to press!

You can find step by step training showing how this and various other strategies work at Anywheretrader.com (see also the links in Chapter 12)

How does the Strategy make money?

This strategy makes money by following trends. It aims to "ride" the trend until it runs out. By looking for possible candidates your chances of finding what you are looking for are increased.

Advantages

An advantage of this strategy is that it can make money from markets and stocks that go down as well as up.

Downsides

A downside is the extra time that this takes. This requires a much more structured approach than the other strategies and a much more pro-active approach.

There is always the risk that the trend "ends" just as you are buying into it. This means that you will have losing trades. In order to make the odds work in your favour you do need to make a number of trades. Since you will be cutting your losses, and letting your profits run for so long as the trend remains intact you should, over time have a good chance of making significant gains.

Because this strategy involves making numerous trades (rather than "setting and forgetting", as you might for strategies one, two or three) it is well worth documenting your trades, what you did, how much you made, what worked and what didn't. You can do this in an excel spreadsheet but for a living "visual" record I would recommend the Visual Trading Journal (which is a paperback journal) in order to document and capture gains and losses. You can find a link to this in Chapter 12.

How does this strategy manage risk?

There are several ways that this strategy manages risk:

The screening process looks to minimise exposure to weak stocks (when placing trades to go up) – or indeed to deliberately seek out weak stocks (for trades going down).

Having a stop loss in place, whilst letting profits run gives a better chance of winning over time and limits losses on each trade to a manageable number.

Moving the stop loss in the direction of the trade means that risk is minimised over time. As soon as possible you are looking to move the stop loss to the purchase price (for trades going up) or "sell to open" price so that everything beyond that is profit, without the risk.

Summary

By following the markets up AND down you can make money in each direction – meaning there's always a trade that's available somewhere.

STRATEGY SIX - REVERSION TO THE MEAN – BUY LOW, SELL HIGH

The polar opposite of the above strategy (which aims at stocks or funds moving quickly up or downwards) in a trend is the sixth strategy.

This seeks to actively seek out stocks that are moving in a channel, hitting similar highs and lows regularly – and looks to buy into the relevant fund or stock at a low price and sell it at a higher price.

The Strategy

The steps are as follows:

1. Screen for stocks and funds as per strategy five. Like strategy five you can look for stocks that are strong (and likely to go up) and for stocks that are weak (and likely to go down).

2. When you find some suitable candidates, look to see if you can find anywhere the stocks are making an obvious "Channel". For this you want two things:

   a. You are looking back at the stock price and looking to see where it makes highs. You are looking to see if there is a "Ceiling" beyond which the stock does not typically go any higher. This area (at which the stock stops rising) is known as "resistance".

b. You are also looking to find an area where the stock comes down to and appears to stop falling, before going back up again. This is known as resistance).

c. Ideally you should see a pattern of highs and lows that are in similar positions (around the same price each time). You can test this by drawing a horizontal line on a chart from any high or low to see if others align with it. If you have found this then you have found a stock that is "Channelling".

(See below for a "Channelling" stock – note that, from October the stock reaches highs of $143 and no higher (resistance), several times and lows (support) of around $136.5).

Look closely and you'll also see another phenomenon that is common with channelling stocks – in October the support is nearer $139 and then that becomes the new "resistance" going forwards from mid-November. This is a channel, within a wider channel.

Here you're looking at the wider picture and looking for the stock to bounce off the resistance and the support several times.

Clickableinsome published on TradingView.com, January 18, 2020 10:43:01 UTC
BATS:GLD, 60 146.58 ▲ +0.27 (+0.18%) O:146.85 H:146.85 L:146.50 C:146.59

3. One important rule – check which way the stock is trending (remember strategy three) when you are searching for candidates to make your opening trade NEVER look to buy when the stock or fund is trending down (i.e. is making lower highs or lower lows. NEVER look to sell to open when the stock or fund is trending up (higher highs or higher lows). Remember – the "trend is your friend" – don't try to go against it.

4. Now for the clever part – you're going to work out the average volatility of the stock – how high and low it typically goes over the past six months and as a result where it is likely to be over the next month. Don't worry – this doesn't involve any maths skills – just an indicator – the "Keltner Channel".

5. On your chart, use this indicator to show where the stock or fund has come to and is predicted to go to, based on the same level of volatility. The indicator, once chosen usually shows a top and a bottom line as well as a middle line. The stock or fund has a high probability of

ending up in the next month between the two lines assuming volatility stays the same.

6. See if the stock price appears to bounce along the bottom line and bounce down from the top line. If so then the indicator is working as it should. You are looking to buy when the stock or fund has "bounced" on the bottom line but is still in the lower half of the channel (below the middle line).

7. Alternatively, if you're shorting the stock you're looking to "sell to open" when the stock or fund has bounced off the top of the channel but is still in the top of the channel (above the middle line).

8. As with the previous strategy – you want to place and keep a stop loss order just below the bottom of the Keltner channel at the time the order was placed (for trades going up) or just above the top of the Keltner channel (for trades going down). Move the stop loss in line with the stock or fund. You don't need to actively sell

– rather your stop loss will kick in when the trend reverses. Again – look to move the stop loss to the purchase price (trends going up) or "sell to open" price (trades going down) as soon as you can to minimise risk.

How does the Strategy make money

This strategy makes money by working out the "range" of a stock or fund -from top to bottom and looks to buy close to the bottom and follow it up to the top of the channel (or in some cases above it).

For short sales the reverse is true – you are looking to "sell to open" when the stock is at the top of its price range, and only buy back the stock once it has dropped in value.

Advantages

This strategy is very visual (the indicator shows the range that you are operating within and makes it easy to see where the top and bottom are).

Unlike other strategies the channel gives you an idea of how much profit you might make on a trade. If the profit is small (because the stock price is already close to the middle of the channel) then you may want to look for a better trade.

Downsides

The Keltner channel, whilst amazingly useful, is not fool proof. As an indicator it relies upon the future being similar to the past. It has no idea about news stories, market sentiment or otherwise. It is merely a calculation that helps work out what the channel could be like. You do therefore need to use stop losses for this strategy.

How does this strategy manage risk?

Screening stocks that are suitable for this strategy already reduces the risk by filtering out weak stocks (for trades going up) or strong ones (for trades going down).

This strategy manages risk by setting out the likely channel – where the stock is likely to go to. Having a stop loss in place (and moving it as the trade goes in the right direction) is important. As with the other strategies - moving the stop loss to the purchase price (for trades going up) or "sell to open" price (for trades going down).

Summary

By following a stock's ups and downs you can work out if it is "cheap" or "expensive" relative to its recent history and can profit from following its likely moves up or down between its recent highs and lows.

STRATEGY SEVEN – USING OPTIONS TO ADD LEVERAGE

So far, you've moved from investing, through trading stocks – now let's move it up a level to trading options.

This strategy uses the same core strategy of reversion to the mean, but uses options rather than stocks. This is one of my favourite strategies as it magnifies the gain whilst minimising the risk.

How do options work?

Options are a way of trading in stocks without having to buy the stock itself. There are two sorts – a "Call" option and a "Put" option.

Whenever you buy a "Call" option contract you are buying the right to buy 100 stocks at a certain price (the "strike price"). If you buy a monthly call option you can buy at this strike price at any point over the following month. You'd do this in order to benefit from the rise in price in the stock. If you think the stock will go up in price (above the strike price) then you might buy a Call option to benefit from the increase in price (at a much lower cost than buying the stocks themselves).

If you were to buy a "Put" option you are buying the right to sell stocks at a certain price. You might do this if you already hold the stocks and think that they are likely to down in price. For the next month, no matter what the stock price does, you know that you can sell at the strike price. This "Put" option then acts as a form of insurance.

Selling options

What we're going to do here however isn't "buying" an option – we're not going to buy an option at all.

Rather we're going to "write" or "sell" an option in place of buying the stock. This means that, for each options contract that we "sell" - we're "selling" the right to either sell stocks to us (in the case of a put option) or the right to buy stocks from us (in the case of a call option).

Unlike the options buyer we don't need the stock to rise or fall in order to make a profit. Rather – we receive an income every time we sell an option. This is known as the options "premium".

I know it might sound odd "Selling" something that you've not had to buy – which is why some people prefer to describe this as "writing" an option. Effectively you are making something from scratch – a promise to the buyer to sell or buy stocks at a certain price.

You will only sell a "Put" option when you have cash but no stocks (and are promising to buy the stocks from the option buyer).

You'll sell a Call option for the stocks if you already own the stocks and are offering to sell your stocks to the option buyer.

The Strategy

The strategy uses the same theory as strategy six, but instead of buying a stock that is going up, you sell a put option on that same stock. Instead of selling short a stock that is going down, you sell a call option on that same stock.

Each time you sell an option you are making a promise to either buy or sell the underlying stock should they fall below a certain price (if selling a put option) or if they rise above a certain price (if selling a call option). It is that promise, made monthly, that we are being paid for.

In each case you are selling options on the underlying security.

The steps are as follows:

1. As per strategy six – screen for stocks that are going up or down.

2. Find one (or several) that fits within the Keltner channel and which has, over the last few months bounced off the bottom and top of the channel.

3. Of these, find a stock that;

    a. Is trending upwards; and

    b. Has just bounced off the bottom of the Keltner channel.

4. Sell a one-month expiry "put" option on the stock. In other words – find a put option that expires in one month's time and "Sell to Open" that put option.

5. When you are looking for the option to sell you will need to decide on the relevant strike price for that option. You will need to choose the strike price (the price at which the option will execute) that is slightly below the bottom of the Keltner channel.

6. Place the order, collect the option premium and wait until the end of the month.

7. At the end of the month one of two things will have happened. Either:

   a. The stock has gone below the "strike price" and executed. In which case you now own the stock; or

   b. The stock has not gone below the "strike price" meaning that that the option expired without executing. In which case you now have the same cash that you started with.

In either case you have received the option premium from step 4.

8. The next step depends whether the previous option executed or not:

   a. If in the previous month the option was not executed then you sell another put option (as per steps 3,4 and 5)

   b. If it did execute, meaning that you now own the security then you now sell a one-month **call option,** with a strike price that is slightly **above** the top of the Keltner channel. Once again you collect the premium and wait for the end of the month.

c. If the call option executes (i.e. the price of the security went above the top of the Keltner channel) then you now are back in cash – you can now sell a put option and repeat steps 3, 4 and 5.

d. If it does not execute but rather expires, then you still hold the security – so can sell another call option the next month, again slightly above the Keltner channel.

If all of the above sounds like so much gobbledygook then this strategy may not yet be for you. I appreciate that this is a more advanced strategy. Trading options adds a layer of complexity that means it is much easier to explain on video than in a book.

You can find a video with more information on this strategy at www.getstartedwithstocks.com and it is a strategy that, because it does take a little more work, does take longer to master.

Hopefully this book gives an idea of how this strategy can make money and why it might be worth exploring. This is certainly one that requires that you first get comfortable with your broker.

How does the Strategy Make Money?

The strategy makes money in two ways. First of all, every month, whether the stock goes up or down you receive a premium for selling the option. This might typically be between 0.5 and 2% per month.

In addition, every so often your Call Option will be exercised (meaning that you will be forced to sell your stocks). As you have set the strike price above the top of the Keltner channel (and bought below the bottom of the Keltner channel) when this happens you also make money from the increase in the value of the stock – however this is a bonus, rather than the focus of the strategy.

Advantages

The advantage of this strategy is that it is relatively low risk. So long as you keep selling put options and those options are not executed – you don't own stocks at all, but are just making money from the promise to buy stocks at a lower price than they are now.

If the option is executed (meaning that you own the stocks) then you continue to make an income no matter which way the stock goes next. You keep taking the monthly options premium. Your risk is limited because you make an income each month regardless of which way the stock goes.

Downsides

One downside is that (as the above explanation might suggest) this does take a little longer to master. It is however well worth the effort.

To sell puts on a stock you must have sufficient cash to be able to afford 100 of the relevant stock per option. That means that you may be limited to using low-cost stocks for this strategy.

You can of course lose money with this strategy, as with the others. In the event that the stock that you are holding (and selling call options against) goes quickly down in price the value of your stock goes down. Unlike some other strategies you cannot easily use a stop loss since, if you have sold an option on the stock then you are obliged to provide the stock if it is exercised. You cannot therefore use stop losses to manage risk. You can however keep selling call options and gaining an income each time you do so.

Someone trading this strategy must therefore have a similar mindset to someone investing in strategy two (the dividend investor), i.e., they must be prepared to hold on to the stocks over the long term, and accept dips in the market for so long as they continue to make a regular income from that stock over time.

How does this strategy manage risk?

This strategy manages risk by making an income every month no matter what. Whilst the value of your investment can drop (and you are not able to use a stop loss for this strategy) you are offsetting the risk by constantly drip-feeding income.

In order for this strategy to work long term you need to pick a stock that will not fall to zero. Technology and biotech companies, whilst they would produce a significant income for this strategy are best avoided. Better choices for this strategy are large ETFs (such as the S & P 500) or a commodity like gold or silver.

Summary

Using options for additional leverage means that you can earn an income every month which is more consistent and gives a higher return than trading stocks. In particular trading options allows a trader to use leverage to increase gains and also reduce risk.

STOCK SCREENING

Various of the above strategies can be carried out using a single Exchange Traded Fund (ETF). Alternatively, however you may wish to choose individual stocks to trade.

Where that is the case, you want to use a screening tool to find stocks or funds that fit your criteria. This can get you a better chance of finding stocks that are rising (i.e. in a "Bull Market") and separating those from stocks or funds that are falling in value (i.e. in a "Bear Market").

The best online tool that I have found, and which is, again, free to use is one called "Finviz". You'll find this at www.finviz.com.

Typing in certain criteria to the screener will show stocks that are more likely to go up long term (and for which you'd hope the stock market will treat them well).

The criteria to use for BULL MARKET stocks (going up) are:
On the first page (Screener):

1. Current Volume over $1 Million

   (Why? Because you want stocks that are highly "liquid" – in other words there are lots of investors in those stocks, meaning that they should move smoothly over time, rather than being moved by a small number of investors.

This also means that the difference between the price at which you buy the stock and the price at which you can sell it (the "spread") is relatively small – which will save you money.

2. Price over $10

    (Same reason as above)

3. Option/Shortable – pick "Optionable"

    (If you want to place an options trade – i.e. strategy 7. Not all stocks have options associated with them, so if you want to place an Options based trade, you'll need a stock that has an option associated with it)

On the tab titled "Technical Settings"

4. 20-day SMA – 20-day SMA above 50-day SMA

    (This compares the 20 day "Simple Moving Average", (as referred to in Strategy three) with the 50-day Simple Moving Average. By screening for this indicator, you are identifying stocks that have recently been moving upwards quickly)

5. 50-day SMA – Price above SMA 50

    (This compares the 50-day Simple Moving Average with the Price and confirms that the price of the stock is still be going up)

Then click on "Charts"

This will bring up several pages of charts. By going through the charts and looking for trends that are heading upwards (strategy 3) you can identify stocks that are in a Bull Market, and which might therefore be suitable candidates for strategy number three (or four).

Next – if you are looking for BEAR MARKET stocks (i.e. those that are going down) you will want to use the following criteria:

On the first page (Screener):

1. Average Volume: Over $1 Million

    (Why? Because you want stocks that are highly liquid that move smoothly over time)

2. Option/Shortable: Pick Optionable AND Shortable

    ("Optionable" - if you want to place an options trade it'll need to have an option associated with it. As we're betting on a downwards trend, we want it to be capable of being shorted)

3. Price – over $20

    (We want the stock to be liquid AND we want room for the stock to fall)

On the "Technical" Page:

1. 20 Day SMA: SMA 20 below SMA 50

2. 50 Day SMA: Price below SMA 50

    (these indicate that the stock is falling quickly and continuing to fall)

Then click on "Charts"

This time you are looking for a downwards trend.

This analysis gives a blunt view of the future of the stock. It weeds out the stocks that are clearly not appropriate and leaves only what is left. What it does not do is tell you when the stock will rise or fall.

What you need to do having done this screening is to compile a list of those stocks where:

1. The above criteria are met

2. They are "trending" in line with the criteria (up for Bull Market stocks, down for Bear Market stocks); and

3. They have started to move in the opposite direction, as if they could be about to "bounce" off the previous low (for rising stocks) or off the previous high (for falling stocks); and

4. They show (or look like they might soon show) a bounce – a move back upwards or downwards.

    Keeping this watchlist helps you to decide which stocks to look for – when trading on the basis of strategies 3,4 or 5 in particular.

Using a screening tool like "Finviz" and keeping a watchlist of likely candidates means that, when you're ready to trade you already know which candidates look the strongest and are in a good position to take action.

PUTTING IT ALL TOGETHER

In this book we've looked at strategies from the very simple (buy and hold/ dividend investing) to the frankly quite advanced (selling put and call options).

There are no prizes for complicating things and the best strategy is likely to be the one that you understand and are happy with.

Before actively trading any of these strategies I would recommend getting a "practice account" with your stockbroker to test out the strategy that you most like the look of. Remember if you do so, to treat the invested (invented) money as if it were real. Only that way will you experience how the strategy really "works" for you.

Once you have chosen a strategy, try it out and see how you feel with it. I'd also recommend (particularly for strategies 4-7) keeping a journal of your results so that you prove for yourself what results you get. If your results are not what you'd like then this journal should help you to identify what is going wrong – or if not you, then it should allow someone else to work out if you are doing something wrong.

Next Steps

How will you put all of this into practice? It's easy enough reading about it in a book (or at least we hope it is) however there really is no substitute for giving it a go (ideally in a practice account with "virtual" money).

Some of the strategies are best explained in a video. You can find a whole series of videos setting out the different strategies here.

By all means practice these strategies yourself, try them out and see which you prefer.

If you'd like to see how these work then I'd encourage you to take a look at "getstartedwithstocks.com" where you'll find bonus information on the different strategies as well as video training.

Thank you for reading. I'd be very grateful of your comments. Please do email me at Richard@getstartedwithstocks.com and I'll do my best to respond as soon as I can.

If you've enjoyed this book or found it useful I'd be very grateful of a review – you can do that here:

In the meantime - good luck with your trading journey – you've got the basics – the rest is up to you!

GLOSSARY

There are a number of terms used in this book which might sound unfamiliar when you first come across them – by way of summary I have set out a definition below.

Buy to Open	An order to "buy" a stock or option to "open" (in other words enter into) a trade
Buy to Close	An order to "buy a stock or option to "close" (in other words exit) a trade. This would be the case if the investor has entered the trade by "selling" a stock or option. This order, once triggered, exits the trade by acquiring the stock or the option that was "borrowed" by the investor
Call Option	An instrument which, if bought – allows the buyer to buy stocks at a certain price over a given period (e.g. each monthly call option for Microsoft stocks would give you the right, but not the obligation to

	purchase 100 stocks of Microsoft at some point over the next month). By Selling (or "Writing") the same Call Option you are offering to sell those 100 stocks to the buyer for a fixed price at any point over the next month, in exchange for a premium
Dividend	A payment made by a company out of its earnings to its stockholders.
ETF	Exchange Traded Fund – a fund that is traded on the stock exchange like a stock , but which represents a whole portfolio of stocks or an index. By way of example the "SPY" Exchange traded fund rises and falls with the S&P 500, allowing an investor to trade the whole of the S & P 500 with one stock. There are ETFs for most sectors and indexes as well as ETFs reflecting the price of silver, gold and other commodities.
Index Fund	Like an ETF a fund that tracks an index allows the investor, at a low cost to buy or sell a whole index. Less flexible than an ETF it is not always

	possible to place all types of order on an Index Fund.
Premium	A payment made by the recipient of an option by the person selling that option.
Put Option	An instrument which, if bought, allows the buyer to sell stocks at a certain price over a certain period (e.g. a month) By selling (or "writing") a put option the investor is making a promise for the period of the option to buy stocks from the option buyer, in exchange for a premium.
Sell to Open	An order to enter into a trade by "selling" the relevant stock or option. This means that the investor first borrows the security from the broker and sells it, with a view to buying it back later at a higher price.
Sell to Close	An order to exit a trade by selling a stock, option or other security. This order can be used by an investor who already owns the relevant stock or option, in order to exit the trade.

Short	When you "short" a stock you are effectively betting that the price will go down. You are committing to buy the stock at some future date (by which time you are hoping that it will be worth less than its current price)
SMA	Simple Moving Average – this is the average price of the stock as worked out over several periods. For example, the 20-day Simple Moving Average is the average stock price of a stock over the past 20 days. On a chart, as well as seeing the stock price you can see how the 20-day average moves over time. It is generally seen as a positive sign (indicating a rising stock price) if a shorter moving average crosses over and moves above a longer moving average (e.g., the 20-day SMA crosses over and moves above the 50-day SMA)
Stocks/Stocks	A "Share" is an instrument trading on an exchange that represents a part ownership of the company. In the UK we talk of "Shares" and "Share trading". In the USA the term used is "Stocks"

	and "Stock trading". There is no difference other than the language.
Stop Loss	An order to sell a stock at the point where it falls by a certain amount. Typically, a stop option is put in place in case the trade goes against the investor, however it can also be used to follow a winning trend in order to allow the investor to follow the trend as far as possible. As the stock goes up in value, any reversal will not wipe out all of the gains but just the most recent increase. A stop loss can be used in either direction and is placed underneath the current price of stocks that have been purchased or above the current price of stocks that have been sold short.
Strike Price	In an option contract the strike price is the price at which the stocks can be sold (in a put contract) or bought (in a Call contract). This is different to the price of the option itself (which is usually a fraction of the value of the underlying stocks).

USEFUL RESOURCES/ FURTHER READING
(LINKS ARE TO AMAZON)

Strategy One	Harry Browne - the permanent portfolio Tony Robbins - Money, Master the Game Reset - David Sawyer Meb Faber - Global Asset Allocation
Strategy Two	Motley Fool – Stephen Bland (see the Motley Fool website and search for the "High Yield Portfolio") Step by step dividend investing
Strategy Three	Trend Following - Michael Covel
Strategy Four	Big Money, Little Effort - Mark Shipman
Strategy Five	The Complete Turtle Trader - Michael Covel
Strategy Six	Marcus de Maria - the Lunchtime Trader

Strategy Seven	Jeremy Dowling – the Successful Trader
All of the above strategies	http://www.getstartedwithstocks.com
Trading Journal	The Visual Trading Journal - Anywhere Trader - R Nicholas

If you found this book useful in any way I would be very grateful if you would consider leaving a review on Amazon

www.ingramcontent.com/pod-product-compliance
Lightning Source LLC
Chambersburg PA
CBHW030954240526
45463CB00016B/2557